Secretum Secretorum

of

Pseudo-Aristotle

Secretum Secretorum of Pseudo-Aristotle

The Secret of Secrets, or in Latin Secretum or Secreta Secretorum is a translation of the Arabic Kitab Sirr Al-Asrar, the Book of the Science of Government, on the Good Ordering of Statecraft.

The prologue of a Doctor in recommendacion of Arystotle the prynce of phylosophers

God almyghty save our kynge, & the glory of all his frendes, and conferme his realme in the faythe of god. And cause hym to reygne in the exaltacyon, prayse and honour of his people. I whiche am servaunt to the kynge have put in execution the werke of his commaundement, in getynge a boke of good maners to his governaunce. The whiche boke is called the Secrete of Secretes, made by the prince of phylosophers Arystotle the sone of Mahonnet of Macedony, to his dysciple the emperour Alexander sone of Phylyp kynge of Macedony the which Alexandre had two crownes. This sayd boke Arystotle compyled in the oldenesse of his body bycause that he might no more travayle nor ryde to do suche besynesses as Alexander had put in to his charge. For Alexandre had made hym governour and mayster above all other bycause he was a man of veray good councell, of grete clerge, and subtyll understanding. And incessantly studyed good & gracyous maners, & scyences spyrytuall, contemplatives, and charytables. He was a wyse man, & meke, lovynge reason and Justyce, & ever reported ryghtwysnesse & trouthe. And therfore many phylosophres repute hym of the nombre of prophetes. And say that they had founde dyvers bokes of the grekes which god had sent hym by his moost excellent aungell, saynge to hym, `I shall make the to be called in the worlde more an aungell than a man.' And wyte ye that Arystotle dyde in his lyfe many sygnes whiche were straunge in werkes & mervayles whiche were to longe to be accompted. Before his dethe he dyde many straunge werkes. Wherfore a relygyon & company peryadyc sayd & helde opynion that he had ben in heven in lykeness of a douve of fyre. And as longe as he lyved Alexander overcame all the worlde through his councell. And all landes by the fame of hym were put under the imperyall commaundement, & in lykewyse they of Perce, & Araby. And there was none that durst gaynsay Alexander, in worde nor dede. And the sayd Arystotle made many goodly epystles for the love that he had to Alexander, & for to cause hym to knowe all the secretes, he made an epystle here under wryten, the which he sent to Alexander. And whan Alexander had overcome the realme of Perce & set the moost of them in his prysons, he sent an epystle to Arystotle whiche foloweth.

An epystle that Alexander sent to Arystotle.

Doctour of Justyce & right noble phylosopher we sygnyfy to thy hygh wysdome, that we have sen in the realme of Perce many men, whiche habounde gretly in reason & understondyng, subtyl & penetratyfe. Wherfore al we have intencyon to put them to deth. Howbeit as thou semest best sygnyfy us by thy lettres.

An epystle that Aristotle sent to Alexander.

Yf thou can moeve & chaunge the ayre frome the erth & water, & the ordynaunce of thy cytees to accomplysshe thy pleasure. Yf thou cannot do it ceas of & do it not, but governe them in thy goodnesse and exalt them in benygnyte. And yf thou do thus I hope with the grace of god that they all shall be thy frendes to all thy good pleasures and commaundements. And for the love that they shall have in the, thou shalt peasybly reygne over them in grete vyctory.

And whan Alexander had red this epystle, he dyde after his councell, and they of Perce were more obedyent to hym than to ony other nacyon.

The prologue of a doctour named Phylyp that translated this boke in to latyn.

Phylyp that translated this boke in to latyn was a chylde of Parys, & was a veray wyse interpretour & understander of languages, & he sayd thus, `I have not knowen nor seen tyme that the phylosophers have holpen, or have ben acustomed to helpe or to make all werkes or all secretes but that I have sought, nor have knowen by no man by whome I knewe that he had knowlegyng of the scryptures of Phylosophers; but I have vysited him unto the tyme that I came to the knowlege of councell, the which was Estulapideus, & a man solytary & of grete abstynence, and veray wyse in phylosophy, to whom I meked me dylynently, requyrynge hym hat he wolde shewe to me the scryptures of the knowlege of the sonne, the whiche he gave unto me, with a ryght good wyll: And surely I founde as moche as I desyred, & all that I had ben about a hole yere, & wherfore I had longe tyme travayled. And I thus havynge my desyre retorned home with grete ioye, yeldyng thankes to god my creatour.

And than at the request of the moost noble kynge with grete study & labour I translated this boke out of Greke language in to Caldees tongue & syth in to the speche of Araby. The which boke the mooste wyse man Arystotle made, whiche andwered alwayes to all the requestes of kynge Alexandre, as more playnly appereth in this present boke.'

An epystle sent to kyng Alexandre by Arystotle.

Ryght glorious sone and ryghtwyse, god conserve the in the walke of knowlegyng the ways of trouthe & vertues, and withdrawe thy carnall and beestly desyres, & conferme thy realme to his servyce, & to thy honour. Letynge the wyte deere sone that I have receyved thyn epystle reverently & honourably as it apperteyneth, and playnly have understande the grete desyre that thou hast that I were personally with the. Reprovynge me of that I care but lytel for thy besynesses. For the which cause I have ordeyned & hasted me to make a boke for the, the which shall weye & conteyne all my werkes, supplyenge myn absence & defautes, and shall be to the a ryght certayne rule & doctryne in all thynges that thou wyllest. The whiche I will shew as I were presently with the. Dere son thou ought not to repreve nor blame me, for thou knowest well that for no thynge of the worlde, but that I would go to the, and yf were not that I am so sore greved, and laden with aege & weykenesse of my persone, wherby in no wyse I can go to the. And wyte thou, that the thynge which thou hast demaunded of me, and that thou so moche desyrest to knowe & have is the secretes that nature humaynes thought scantly can compryse nor susteyne. How than may in the hert of mortall man be wryten or understande that thynge that he ought not to knowe. And that thyng that is not behovefull nor covenable to be spoken of. Howbeit I am bounde by veray duety to answere to that, that thou demaundest. I shall never other thynge shewe the, but that which is wryten in this boke. For yf thou rede it dylygently, and understande it playnly, and that thou mayse knowe that is conteyned in it, without doubt thou shalt have all that that thou desyrest. For god shall gyve the suche grace, suche understandynge, and subtylte of grete wyt and scyence, and also by the doctryne that I have gyven the afore tyme, that by thy selfe thou mayst knowe & conceyve that whiche thou desyrest. And the cause why that I have opened and related my secretes fyguratyvely

& somewhat derkly, & that I have put obscure examples, and by fygures, is that I doubt, & feare moche that this boke sholde come to the handes of infect persones, & in the power of arrogant & evyll folkes, which myght knowe the secretes of god. And god knoweth wel that they be not worthy. Certaynly I make grete doubt, that I in this trespace not the wyll and the grace of god. I do relate & dyscover this thynge, as it hath ben revelate of god unto the. Wyte thou then ryght dere sone that I have dyscovered to the, the thynges that ben to be hyd. And yf thou dyscover these secretes, thou shalt have shortly evyl fortunes, and mayst not be sure frome grete harmes that shall be comynge towarde the. But almyghty god kepe the & me from suche thynges, & from all dyshonest thynges. And after all these thynges have in thy mynde this noble & prouffytable doctryne, that I make redy to the, & intende to expose thy noble hert, to informe it to thy grete solace, as myrour of helth yf thou wylt apply the therto. Moost dere sone it behoveth every kyng to have two thynges to sustayne hym & his royalme. But he maye not stedfastely have it, but yf he have good & grete governaunce of them that ought to governe. And he that reygneth so is obeyed one of his subgectes. And his subgectes egally with one courage, & by one selfe forme shalbe obedyent to the lorde. For by the dysobedyence of the subgectes the power of the lorde is gretly feblysshed. And yf the subgectes reygne, the governaunce may nothyng do. And I shall shewe the, the cause wherfore the subgectes ben styred & couraged to obey theyr lorde. Two thynges ther is. The one is outwarde & the other inwarde. It is not longe syth I declared to the that that is outwarde. That is to wyte, whan the lorde spendeth wysely his rychesse among his subgectes, and that he in them worke lyberalyte & that he gyve to echone as they be worthy. And therwith the kynge behoveth to have a wyle, wherof I shall make mencyon in the chapytre of vyces & helpes. That is so wyte that the kynge ought to enforce hym to get the hertes of his subgectes by good werkes. And this is the fyrst degre & foundacyon in doyng of his dedes by .ij. thynges. One inward & the other outwarde. The cause outwarde is that the kynge do, & maynteyne Justyce, the possessions & rychesses of his subgectes, & that he be pyteous & mercyfull. The cause inwarde is that he honoure grete lerned men, & that he have them for recommended. For god hath recommended them theyr scyence. And I recommende the this secrete pryncypally with dyvers other, whiche thou shalt fynde in other chapytres of this boke, wherein thou shalt fynde grete wysdome & doctrine & the content of the of the fynal cause wherby thou shalt fynde thy pryncypall purpose. For in it thou shalt lerne the sygnyfycacyions, of the wordes, & obscurytees of the examples. Than thou shalt playnly & perfytely have that, that thou desyrest. Wherfore pray to god moost wyse & gloryous kynge that he wyll lyghten thy reason & understandynge to thende that thou mayst knowe & perceyue the secretes of this scyence. And in the same thou mayst be myn heyre & successour, & that he wyl graunt the largenesse of goodes, to gyve haboundaunce to the lyvyng of wyse men & studyentes, with grace to knowe that which is dyfficyle, & without the same nothyng can be done.

Of the maner of kynges as touchyng largesse.

There be .iiij. maner of kynges. There is a kynge that is lyberall to hym selfe, & lyberall to his subgectes. There is a kynge that is lyberall to hym selfe & havyng to his subgectes. The Ytalyens say that it is no vyce to a kynge that is havynge to hymselfe, & lyberal to his subgectes. The Indyens say that the kyng is good that is hauyng to hymself, & to his subgectes. The Percyens say the contrary, & ben of opynyion that the kyng is not worthy that is not large to hymselfe & havyng to his subgectes. But among all the kynges above sayd it is the worst, & ought in no thynge to be praysed that is not liberall to hym selfe & to his subgectis. For he that is havynge to hym selfe & to his subgectis, his realme shall be clene destroyed. That it behoveth us to enquere of the vertues & vyces abovesayd, & to shew what thyng largesse is, & wherin the errour of largesse lyeth, & what harmes come for lacke of largesse. It is evydent that the qualytees ben to be reproved whan they go fro the meane, & be avarycyous or folysshe lyberall. But yf thou wyll enquere or seke largesse, regarde & consyder thy power, and the tyme of the necessyte, & the merytes of men. And than thou aught to gyve as thy power wyll (by measure) to them that have nede, & be worthy of it. For he that gyveth other wyse he breketh the rule of largesse & synneth. And he that gyveth his goodes to hym that hath no nede, he getteth no thankes. And al that he gyveth to them that be not worthy, is lost. And he that spendeth his goodes outragyously, shall soone come to the wylde brymmes of poverte, & is lyke hym that gyveth victory to his enemyes over hym. But a kynge that gyveth his goodes mesurably to them that have nede, is lyberall to himselfe and his subgectes. And his realme shal come to grete prosperyte, & his commaundement shalbe fulfylled. And he that spendeth the goodes of his realme without ordre, & gyueth to them that be not worthy, & to them that have no nede, such a kynge destroyeth his people, & the comyn welthe, & is not worthy to reygne as a kyng. And the name of avaryce is an over foule name to a kyng, & to moche harme cometh to his regall mageste. Therfore yf a kyng wyl reygne honourably, hym behoveth not to have the one nor the other of these vyces, that is to wyte, that he be not to lyberall, nor to coveytous. And yf the kyng wyl be counceyled, he ought with grete dylygence to pourvey him of a wyse man, whiche shall be chosen amonge all other, to whome he shall commyt his doynges of the realme, & the gouernaunce of the rychesses of the same as they ought to be spent.

Of largesse and avaryce, and of many other vyces.

Kynge Alexander moost dere sone I tell the certaynly that yf ony make greter expence than his relme can susteyne, that he enclyneth to folysshe largesse & avaryce. Suche a kynge without doubt shalbe destroyed. But yf he inclyne to lyberalyre, he shall have perpetuall glory of his realme, yf he drawe hym fro takynge the goodes and possessyons of his subgectes. And wyte thou dere sone that I fynde wryten of a grete doctour named Hermogynes whiche sayth that the gretest & soverayne goodnesse, bryghtnesse of understandyng, & plente of lawe, scyence & perfeccyon of a kynge, is that it behoveth to kepe hym fro takynge of the goodes and possessyons of his subgectes. It hath ben the undoynge of many realmes. For dyvers kynges have made greter & outragyous expences than the stynt of theyr realmes coude extende, wherfore they toke the goodes and landes of theyr subgectes. For the whiche injuryes doynge the people cryed to god, whishe sent vengeaunce on the sayd kynges. In suche wyce that theyr people rebelled agaynst them & put them to destruccyon. And without the grete mercy of god that susteyned them the realmes shold have ben utterly destroyed with the people. Thou then oughtest to absteyne the from outragyous expences, & ought to kepe temperaunce in lyberalyte. And gete not the derke secretnesse & reproches that thou shalt have, for it belongeth not to them that be good.

Of vertues & vyces, & of the doctryne of Arystotle.

The substaunce of all vertuous reygnyng is to gyve to them that be good, & perdon injuryes, honoure & bere reverence to them that be worthy, & have mynde of them that be meke, & amende the defawtes of them that be symple, & with good wyl save the people, & kepe the fro to moche spekyng, let injuryes pass tyll thou se the tyme of defence that thou knowe not the foly of foles. Dere sone I have taught the & shal teche the many thynges the whiche thou shalt kepe in thy hert. And I ensure the that the sayd techynges shall always be there in al thy doynges & werkes. Bryght & suffycyent scyence of physyke shortely comprysed thou shalt have. And I wolde never have shewed the ony thynge, but that the sayd scyence with the techynges that folowe ought to suffyse the & thy werkes in this worlde and in the other.

Of the understandynge.

Dere sone knowe thou that the understandynge is the chyef of the governaunce of man & helth of the soule, keper of vertues, & of vyces. For in the says understandynge we beholde the thynges that be to be chosen. It is the key of vertues, & the rote of all laudable goodes. And the best instrument therof is to have good fame. And yf it be contraryly done, it shalbe confounded at the last by yll fame. A kynge ought pryncypally seke to have a good fame. More for the governynge of his reame than for hymselfe.

Of the fynall intencyon that a kynge ought to have.

For the begynnynge of largesse that a kynge ought to have, is to have good fame, wherby the grete realmes & grete lordysshyppes be goten. And yf thou desyrest to get realmes of lordysshyppes, yf it be not by good fame, thou shalt get none other thynge but envy. And envy bredeth lesynges, whiche is mater and rote of all vyces. Envy bredeth yll speche, yll speche bredeth hate: hate bredeth injustyce, injustyce bredeth batayle, batayle breketh all lawe, dystroyeth cytees, and is contrary to nature. Than thynke dere sone & set thy desyre to get good fame, and thou shalt have in the trouth, & all thynges laudable, for it is cause of al welth. For it is contrary to lesynges, whiche is mater of all vyces, as it is sayd. And trouth engendreth the desyre of Justyce. Justyce engendreth good faythe. Good faythe engendreth famylyaryte. Famylyaryte engendreth frendshyp. Frendshyp engendreth councel and helpe. And for this cause all the worlde was ordeyned, & the lawes made which be covenable to reason and nature. It appereth than that the desyre to have good fame is honourable and perdurable lyfe.

Of evylles that folowe flesshely desyre.

Alexander fayre sone leve thy beestly desyres of thy flesshly appetyte, for they be corruptibles. The flesshely desyres draweth thy hert to beestly corrupcyon of the soule without ony dyscrecyon, & dryeth the body of man. Wotest thou what flesshely love bredeth? It bredeth avaryce, avaryce bredeth desyre, desyre bredeth rychesse, and maketh a man without care, to be a proude man, without lawe, and a thefe. Theft bryngeth a man to shame, and fynall destruccyon of his body.

Of the wysdome and ordynaunce of a kynge.

It is behovefull and ryght that the good fame of a kynge, be in honourable scyence and worthynesse (throughout al realmes) to be shed frome his realme, and have communycacyon of theyr wyse councel with his. And therby he shall be praysed, honoured, & doubted of his subgectes, whan they se that he speketh and doth his werkes wysely. For easely is perceyved the wysdome or foly of a kynge, for whan he governeth hym in worthynesse towarde his subgectes, he is worthy to reygne honourably. But he that putteth his realme in servytude or thraldom, of evyll customes, he breketh the way of veryte. And dyspyseth the good way and lawe of god. And at the last be dyspraysed of all folkes, as he hath deserved.

Of the worthynes, relygyon, and holynesse of a kynge.

And yet agayne well beloved sone I tell the that the phylosophres have spoken and sayd. It behoveth that the royall mageste be governed by ryghtwysnesse, & not by faynt apparence, but in dede, to thende that every man may se and knowe clerely the goodnesse of a kynge, and that he feare god. And wyll be governed in godly wayes, than shall he be honoured & doubted. And yf he shewe hym selfe faynynge to be good, and is nought to his subgectes, his yll werkes can not be hyd, nor it may not be but his people shall knowe it. He shall be dyspysed of god & shamed in the worlde. And his dedes shalbe lessed, & the honoure of the crowne of his realme shall fayle. What shall I tell the more? there is no tresure in this world to good fame. And moreover dere sone, it besemeth that thou worshyp clerkes, and poverte of good men of relygyon, and exalt wyse men and speke oft with them. And questyon often of doubtes with them. And demaunde many thynges of them. And answer wysely to theyr questyons. And honoure noble men as eche of them is worthy.

Of the pourveyaunce of a kynge.

It behoveth that a wyse kynge thynke often of thynges to come that he may provyde for suche thynges as be contrary to hym. And that he may the easlyer bere the adversytees and contrary adventures. And the kyng ought to be wysely hyd, & refreyned, to thende that without delyberacyon he come not to the dede that he purposed in his anger. And he ought reasonably knowlege his anger and errour, and appease hym selfe easely. For the moost soverayne wysdome and vertue that a kynge may have, is to rule himselfe wysely. And whan he seeth ony thynge that is good and prouffytable for hym to be done, he sholde do it with grete dylygence, & dyscrecyon bycause the people shal not say that he hath done his besynesse folysshely, or to neglygently.

Of the vestymentes of a kynge.

It besemeth well to the mageste royall that the kynge be clothed honourably. And that he shewe hymselfe alway in fayre and royall clothes. And ought in beaute of robbes to surmount all other clothynge. Also he ought with grete prerogatyf & dygnyte use fayre, deere, & straunge vestures. For therby is his dygnyte more excellent and his myght more exalted. And more reverence is made to hym. And also it besemeth a kynge to be fayre spoken, with softe and kynde wordes, specyally in tyme of warre.

Of the countenaunce of a kynge.

Swete sone Alexander it is a goodly thyng precyous, and honourable whan the kynge speketh but lytell. But yf over grete nede requyre it. It is better that the eeres of the people be wylling to here the wordes of a kynge, than to be wery of his to moche spekyng. For whan the eeres be glutted with the kynges speche theyr hertes be wery to se hym. And also the kynge ought not to shewe hymselfe to often to his people, nor haunt to moche the company of his subgectes, & specyall of vylayns. And therfore the Yndyens have a good custome in the ordynaunce of theyr realme. For theyr maner is that theyr kynge sheweth hymselfe but ones in the yere. And than he is clothed in vesture royall. And all the barons and knyghtes of his realme ben rychely armed and arayed about hym. And he is set upon a stede the ceptre in his hande armed with ryche armures royalles, and all his people a good way before the barons & other noble men. And ther they shew the dyuers perylles & adventures that be passed. And how that he & his councell is well ordred. And the kynge as than is wonte to pardon grete offences to some of them. And whan the parlyament is ended the kynge setteth hym in a chayre & anone ryseth one of the moost wysest men & speketh to the people, praysyng & commendyng the wyt & good governaunce of the kynge. In yeldynge thankes to god that hath so well ruled and maynteyned the Yndyens kynge, & that they are pourveyed of so wyse & honourable a kynge to reygne & guyde them. And then he confermeth the sayd people in one wyl & courage to the obedyence of the kynge. And then he commendeth the people & aloweth them gretly of theyr good maners & condicyons which be reporteth do them. And sheweth them goodly wordes & examples, the better to put them in grace & obeysaunce, with mekenesse in the good wyll of the kynge. And whan this wyse prynce hath thus spoken, the people enforce them to exalte the praysynges, and commendacyons, and good maners of this sayd kynge, in prayenge god hertely for hym. And by this meane by theyr good maners and wysdome of theyr kyng they cause countrees and cytees to be obedyent to them. And thus ben the chyldren brought up in theyr youth, & taught in the honoure and revernence of the kynge. And the good fame of the kynge secretly and manyfestly is spredde and knowen. And the ryche and poore ben therby susteyned thoroughout the realme of Ynde. And the kynges possessyons and trybutes encreaseth therby.

Of the Justyce of a kynge.

A Kynge ought to ordre hym soo that he do no wronge, nor harme to marchauntes, but ought to cherysshe them. For they go thoroughout all the worlde, and by them is reported the good and all renownes of lordes & prynces. And a kynge ought by veray Justyce to yelde every man his. And so his landes and cytees shal be garnysshed with all welthes. And the kynges werkes shall multyply to his honoure and glory, and shal be the more redoubted of his foes, and shall lyve & reygne at his wyl & desyre in quyetnesse.

Of the worldly desyres of a kynge.

Alexander ryght worthy sone, coveyt not alwayes worldly thynges, for they be corruptyble. And thynke that thou must leave all. Demaunde than suche thynges as can not be corrupte. That is the lyfe that can not chaunge and the relme perdurable. And reyse thy thoughts in goodnesse, and therin kepe the stronge & gloryous. And leave the lyfe of bestes that alwaye lyve in theyr fylthynesse. Beleve not lyghtly al thynge that is tolde to the. And be not enclyned to pardon them, agaynst whome thou hast had vyctory. And thynke of the tyme & of thynges that may happen. For thou knowest what is to come. And set not thy desyres in meates & drynkes, in lechery, nor to moche slepe, nor in carnall desyres.

Of the chastyte of a kynge.

Soverayne Emperour enclyne not to lechery of women, for it is a swynysshe lyfe. And no glory shall be to the yf thou governe the after the lyvynge of bestes without reason. Dere sone beleve me, for without doubt lechery is destruccyon of the body, the abregement, & corrupcyon of all vertues, the deth of a man self, and maketh the man feminyne. And at the last bryngeth hym to all evylles.

Of the sportynge of a kynge.

Sothly it is besemynge to a kynge to take his pastyme and sporte
with his prynces and lordes. And that he have many and dyvers
maners of mynstrylles, and syndry instrumentes, daunces and
songes. For the humayne creature naturally anoyeth. And in suche
instrumentes and pastymes nature delyteth & the body taketh
force & vygoure. Than yf thou wylt delyte in suche thynges, do it
the moost honestly & secretly that thou mayst. And whan thou
arte in thy pastymes beware for drynkynge of wyne. And let the
other sporte them as longe as they lust. And than thou shalte have
many secrets dysclosed. And make not this pastyme often, but
twyse or thryse in the yere. Also it behoveth the to have nyghe to
the some of thy famylyer servauntes that shal tel and reporte to
the what is sayd in the realme. And whan thou arte amonge thy
barons & subgectes, honoure wyse men & bere reverence to every
man as they be worthy. And every man in his estate, mayntene &
let them ete with the somtyme, one after another. And gyve
gownes somtyme to one & somtyme to another, after theyr estate,
and as they be worthy. And in ony wyse se that there be none of
thy knyghtes & famylyers, but that he fele of thy lyberalyte & of
thy grace. And thus overall shall appere thy largesse & gretnesse of
thy courage and honour.

Of the dyscrecyon of a kynge.

Most worthy sone it is good that a kynge have lyberalyte, goodly gesture, and countenaunce, & that he laughe not to moche. For overmoche laughyng causeth many to be lesse set by, and to be lesse honoured. And fynably overmoch laughyng maketh a person to seme older than he is. Also a kynge ought to love his people in his courte and of his councel more than in other partyes. And yf ony do vylany to another, he ought to punysshe hym as he hath deserved, that other may take example therby, and eschewe them from yll doynge. And in that punysshynge thou ought to regarde the persone that hath done amysse. For elles sholde a hyghe & noble man be punysshed as another. And yf thou do so thou shalt not be alowed of the people. And it is good somtyme to do rygorous & strayt Justice, & somtyme noe, to thende not that dyfference of the persones be knowen. For it is wryten in the boke of Machabees that a kynge ought to be praysed & loved, yf he be lyke the eygle, which hath lorshyp over all fowles. And not as he which wyll be lyke another foule that is subgecte to the eygle. Wherfore yf ony do vylany to ony other in the presence of the kynges mageste, it ought to be regarded & consydered yf the offence were done in game or for to cause the kyng to laugh, or to make hym or other glad of it, or yf he dyde it in despyte, & shame of the mageste royall. For the fyrst dede he ought to be correcte, and for the seconde to suffre dethe.

Of the reverence of a kynge.

Worthy kynge Alexander dere sone the obedyence to a kynge cometh by iiij. thynges. That is for the vertuous lyvynge of the kynge. Bycause he maketh hym to be beloved of his subgectes. Bycause he is curteys. And for the honoure and reverence, that he doth to them that be moost worthy of it. My dere sone do so moch that thou mayst drawe to the the courages of thy subgectes, and avenge them of all wronges & injuryes done to them. And beware that thou gyve not to thy subgectes cause and mater to speke agaynst the. For speche of people many tymes may do hurt. Than have in thy mynde suche wyse that nothyng may be sayd agaynst the. And so thou shall eschue the yll wyl and dedes of them that had yll wyll agaynst the. And forsoth the largenesse of the glory of thy dygnyte and reverence, and exaltacyon of thy realme, and that reboundeth moost to thy honoure is to have the hertes of thy subgectes. It is founde in holy scryptures, that the kyng is over a realme as the rayne is over the erth which is the grace of god and blyssynge of the hevens and cometh on the erthe, and all lyvynge creatures. For the rayne is called the way of marchauntes, and helpe of buylders. How be it that in the rayne falleth somtyme thondre and lyghtnynge, swellynge of the see, and floodes with tempestes and many other evyls cometh therby, wherwith medowes and verdures hath perysshed. For god made it so of his grete goodnesse, benygnyte, and grace. The which selfe example ye may fynde in wynter and somer. In the whiche the soverayne largesse gyveth and ordeyneth coldenesse and heate, engendrynge and encreasynge of all newe thynges. How be it many evyls & perylles cometh by the rygour of grete coldenesse of wynter, & grete heates of somer. In lyke wyse dere sone is it of a kynge. For many tymes the kynge doth many grefes and evylles to his subgectes, and maketh them to beare grete herte agaynst hym. But whan the people seeth that by the grace and good governaunce of the kynge they be in peas and well ruled they forgete the abovesayd evylles, and thanke the gloryous god that hath pourveyed them of so wyse a kynge.

How the kynge ought to remembre his subgectes.

I requyre the swete sone that thou of thy goodnesse thynke and inquyre oftentymes of thy poore subgectes, and knowe theyr necessytees. And set amonge them suche men as be vertuous and that loveth god and Justyce and that knoweth theyr maners, and understandeth theyr speches, and can governe them peasybly and in love. And yf thou do thus, thou shalt do the pleasure of thy creatoure. And it shall be saufegarde to thy realme, and gladnesse of the and thy people.

Of the mercy of a kynge.

Dere sone I concell the that thou make grete provysyon of corne and vytayles in such wyse that thy countrees may have haboundaunce, in eschewynge (as it chaunceth often) to have scarcyte, and famyn. In so moche that by the grete prudence thou mayst save and maynteyne thy subjects, and thout ought to have thy garners stuffed, and to proclayme thrughout all thy realme and cytees, how thou hast gadred and stored the of greynes and other vytayles. And that thou kepest them to the provysyon of thy realme, and to utter them with plente to the salvacyon of thy subgectes. The which doynge wyll cause thy people to be coragyous to do thy commaundementes. And so thou shalt prospere, and every man wyll meruayle of thy grete lyberalyte, & of the provydence afore hande in thy besynesses. And they wyll repute the as holy, and lawde and magnyfye thy worthynesse. And every man wyll feare to dysplease the.

Of paynes and punysshementes.

My dere sone Alexander, I admonysshe, and also praye the to kepe my doctrynes and thou shalt come to thy purpose. And thy realme shall be durable and in good estate. That is to wyte, above all thynge that thou kepe the frome shedynge of mannes blode. For it belongeth onely to god, whiche knoweth the secretes of men. Than take not on the, the offyce that belongeth onely to almyghty god, wherfore as moche as thou mayst withdrawe thy hande therfro. For the doctour Hermogenes sayth, that who that sleeth the creature lyke unto hym, all the sterres of the skye ceaseth not to crye to the mageste of god, lorde, lorde, thy servaunt wyll be lyke unto the. For surely god wyll take vengeaunce on hym that sleeth a man, and specyally without reasonable cause. For god answereth to the vertues of heven saynge, Leave ye, for in me lyeth the vengeaunce, and I can yelde it. And wyte thou that the vertues of heven without cease do present before the face of god, the dethe and blode of hym that is deed, tyll that god hath taken vengeaunce for it.

Of the knowlege of the sayd paynes.

O moost lovynge sone, of all suche paynes with the knowlege therof, wyte thou that I have sene moche harme, and many evylles oftentymes come therby. Do soo that thou mayst have in thy mynde the dedes or werkes of poetes. And thynke how they have lyved. And therby thou mayst se and lerne many goodly examples. And theyre thoughtes shal gyve the grete documentes in tyme comynge. And also I pray the my dere sone, that thou greve nor dysprayse none lesser than thou. For it happeneth often that the small estate ryseth ryght soone in to grete rychesses and honoures, and may be so myghty that he maye endomage the. Many examples therof hath ben seen as phylosophres reherse.

How a kynge ought to kepe his fayth or othe.

Above all thynge (dere sone) beware that thou breke not thy faythe and othe that thou hast made. For it is belongynge to strompettes, and also to people that kepe not, nor do not care for theyre faythe and othe. Wherfore kepe thy faythe that thou hast promysed, for and yf that thou do otherwyse, it wyll come to an evyll ende at the last. And yf by adventure or fortune, it chaunceth that ony welthe cometh by faythe brekynge, the trust therof sholde not be good, but veray evyll & reprovable, and suche a man is put in the nombres of them that be nought. Wyte thou then that by kepynge of faythe is made the goodly assemblynge of men. Cytees ben inhabyted with comyns, and soo is the good sygnouryes of kynges. By kepynge of fayth castelles ben holden and kepte in lordships. And yf thou breke thy fayth thou shalt be reputed of every man as a chylde or a brute beest than beware therof. And kepe also the others, and alyaunces that thou hast made, though that they be grevous and domageable to the. Wotest thou not that thou hast two spyrytes alwaye with the, one on the ryght syde and the other on the lyft syde, whiche knowe and kepe all thy workes. And report to thy creatoure al that thou hast done. Of a trouth thou ought onely to absteyne the frome all dyshonest workes. And constreyne none to swere, but he be moche requyred and prayed. And yf thou wylt wyte what was the destruccyon of Nubye, and of the assyryens. I certyfye the that theyr kynge made othes gylefully, to deceyve the men and cytezens next by. And brake his alyaunces and promysses that he had made, bycause they were profytable to his realme. And also to his subgectes he made many fals othes to destroy theyr next neyghboures. The ryghtwyse Juge coude susteyne nor suffre them no longer. Moost dere sone I wyll that thou knowe, that for the governynge and ordynaunce of thy realme I have made the some new doctrynes, the whiche specyally is for the profyte of thyn owne famylyers and the. But as yet it is not tyme to gyve them to the. I wyll gyve the them in a certayne place of this boke shortly abreged. The which yf thou kepe for thy selfe prouffytably, with the helpe of god thou shalt have prosperyte, and that that thou desyrest. Swete sone repente the not of thynges that be passed, for that belongeth to women whiche ben weyke of condycyon. Let thy goodnesse, thy faythfulnesse, and conscyence be all hoole, and manyfest. And they shall be saufegarde of thy realme and destruccyon of thyn enemyes.

Of studye.

Take hede that thou have studyes and scoles in thy cytees. And cause all thy people to lerne theyr chyldren lettres and noble scyences, and use them to studye. For thou ought to helpe and socoure the governayle of studyes and poore scolers. And gyve avauntages and prerogatyves to good studyentes that proufyte to theyr lernynge, and this wyse thou shalt gyve an example to them that be laye, exalte theyr prayers and receyve theyr wrytynge mekely, prayse them that ought to be worshipped. Gyve thy goodes to them that be worthy. Cherysshe clerkes and styre them to prayse the. And put the and thy werkes in goodly wrytynges, which by them shalbe perpetually praysed.

How a kynge ought to kepe his body.

Most beloved sone kynge Alexandre, trust not in women, nor in theyr werkes, nor servyces, and company not with them. And yf necessyte were that thou must have company of a woman, do so that thou mayst knowe that she is true to the, and holsome of her bodye. For whan thy persone is betwene the armes of a woman, thou arte as a Jewell put, and restynge in the handes of a marchaunt, that careth not to whome it is solde. And beynge betwene her handes, is the poyson of thy welfare, and also the destruccyon of thy body. Beware therfore dere sone, of suche women, for they be venymous and deedly. For it is no newe thynge to knowe that by theyr venym many men have dyed. Thou knowest well that many kynges have forthered and shortened theyr lyves and have dyed by poyson. Also dere Alexander beware that thou put not thy truse in one physycyen onely. For one physycyen maye hurte the, and shortely do the moche harme. And therfore yf thou mayse, do so that thou have many physycyens. And that they be of one agrement. And yf thou wylt have ony medycyn, take it not but by the councell of them all. And that they be such as knoweth the qualyte and nature of the thynges that ben put, and necessary in the medycyne. And that it be of a certayne weyght and measure, as the medycyne requyreth it. For by equall porcyons of weyght and measure the arte of physyke is compownded. And thynke on dere sone that whan thou was in the partyes of Ynde, many people made to the grete presentes and fayre. Amonge the whiche was sente a fayre mayden whiche in her chyldheed had be nourysshed with venym of serpentes, werby her nature was converted in to the nature of serpentes. And than yf I had not wysely beholden her and by my artes and wyt knowen her, bycause that contynually, and without shamefastnesse ever she loked in the faces of the people, I perceyved that with ones bytynge she wolde have put a man to deth as sythen thou hast seen the experyence before the. And yf I had not knowen her nature, at the fyrst tyme that thou had medled with the sayd mayden thou haddest ben deed without remedy. Fayre sone kepe thy noble soule, whiche is gyven to the and sent from the company of aungelles the whiche is taken to the of god for to kepe. Not that thou soyle & marre it, but that it be put amonge the wyse & gloryfyed spyrytes.

Of the dyfference of astronomy.

Alexander fayre sone, I praye the, that yf thou mayst do it, that thou ryse not, nor eate, nor drynke, nor do ony other thynge, but by the councell of some that knoweth and hath the scyence in knowlegynge the sterres and astronomye. And thou shalte wyte my dere sone that almyghty god hath made nothynge without cause, but hath done every thynge reasonably. And by certayne scyences and wayes, the wyse phylozopher Platon sought and felte the operacyons of all thynges composed of the foure elementes, and the humoures contrayres. And hadde also the knowlege of the thynges created and formed. And also my dere sone Alexander I praye the beleve not such fooles which say that the scyence of the planettes is so harde to be knowen, & that none maye come therto. Surely they be fooles and wote not what they say. It is a noble thyng to know thynges whiche be to come. Yf thou knowest the thynges whiche be to come, thou and other persones may put remedy by good prayers. And requyre the creatoure that hath ordeyned them to retourne theyr malyce, & ordeyne them otherwyse. Thynke not dere sone that god hath ordeyned & predestynate such thynges, but that by his power he may chaunge them otherwyse when he pleaseth. Wyte thou dere sone that the good people pray to our creatoure with orysons & devout petycyons, by fastyng & sacrefyces, by almesse & other maner, axyng of pardon of theyr synnes, & doynge penaunce, that our lorde may retorne & remembre suche predestynacyons whiche other do feare so moche. Retorne we dere sone to our fyrst purpose, wite thou that astronomye is devysed in .iiij. partes. That is to wyte in ordynaunce of sterres. In the dysposycyon of sygnes, & of theyr elongacyons. Of the moevynge of the sonne. And this partye is called astronomy. And is the worthyest, of sterres, planettes, and sygnes. And there is .M.xxviij. planettes sygned, and formed, of the whiche we shall speke more playnly.

Of the governayle of helth.

Helthe amonge all thynges is to be goten and hath more than ony myght of rychesses. For the kepyng of helth is by usynge of equal thyngs conjoyned to the body, as by attemperance of humoures. For the gloryous god hath ordeyned them, and gyven dyvers remedyes to the attemperaunce of the humoures to the kepyng of helth. And hath shewed it to his holy men and prophetes, & to many other Just men whiche he dyde chuse and enlumyned with the holy goost, in his sapyence dyvyne, and myghty. And hath gyven them the gyftes of the scyence, of these thynges here after folowynge. That is to wyte they of Ynde, of Grece, and of Athenes. Whiche phylosophres were Just and perfyte, and theyr wrytynges were the begynnynge of scyence & secretes. For in theyr wrytynges is nothynge founde to be reproved nor splyt, but approved of all wyse men.

Of the governayle of seke people.

All wyse and naturall phylosophres say that man is made and composed of foure contrary humours, the which have alway nede to be susteyned with meate and drynke. The substaunce wherof behoveth to yssue and be corrupte yf ony do alway eate and drynke, and he sholde waxe weyke and fall in grete dyseases, and have many inconvenyences. But yf he eate and drynke temperatly and reasonable, he shall fynde helpe of lyfe, strength of body, and helth of all the members. The wyse phylosophres saye that yf any man trespace the god of nature, and the good maner of lyvynge, be it in to moche eatyne and drynkynge, or to moche slepynge, or wakynge, in to moche walkyng or restynge, beynge to laxatyfe, or to moche letynge of blode or to lytell, it can not be but he must fall in many dyseases, and greves. Of the whiche dyseases I have bryefly founde, and therin wyll I shewe the my councell, & remedye for the same. All wyse phylosophres accordeth in one sayeng. Who so kepeth hym fro overmoche eatynge & drynkyng & frome that excesses aforesayd & kepeth temperaunce, he shal be helthfull of his bodye, & lyve longe. For I can fynde no man but he is of this opynyon, & wyll saye that all delectable thynges of the worlde, be it in pleasure of the body, it is but for to lyve the longer in them. But for a more secrete ye ought to enforce you to do suche thynges as ben belongynge to longe lyfe, & not to folowe the appetyte, that is to wyte, not to lye meate upon meat. And dere sone I have herde often spoken of Ypocras which kept many tymes dyete to thende that he myght lyve & endure the longer. Not for to lyve and endure for the meate & drynke. Also dere sone it is grete holsomnesse to be purged of superfluytees & evyll humours whiche ben in the body.

In how many maners a man may kepe his helthe.

Good sone I praye the have in thy mynde stedfastly these certayne instruccyons and kepe them. Knowe thou that helth is chyefly in two thynges. The fyrst is lete a man use suche meates & drynkes as he hath ben nourysshed with. The seconde that he purge hym of yll humours that be corrupte & greve him. For the body of man is fedde with meates & drynkes whiche nourysshe it by naturall heate that dryeth, nouryssheth and fedeth the moystnesse therof.

Of dyvers meates for the stomake.

Whan the body is fat & full of vapours grosse meates is good for it. & of the nourysshyng of suche a body, the dygestyon is grosse, & of grete quantyte for the great heate, & vapours of the the body. And whan the bodye is sklender & drye, subtyll & moyste meates be good for it. And the dygestion therof is of smal quantyte for the stryctnesses of the conduytes. And it is grete wysdome & scyence for a man to use suche meates as been good & appertenent to his complexyon, that is to wyte yf he fedde hym with hote meates temperatly. But yf the heate be to grevous & brennynge within the body by over stronge wynes & hote meates, or other accydentes, than contrary meates & drynkes wyl do grete ease & prouffyte, that is to wyte suche as ben colde.

Of the stomake.

Yf thy stomake be to hote than hote & cours meates be good. For
such a stomake is lyke a myghty fyre for to brenne gret weyght of
logges. But whan the stomake is colde & feble than it is good to
have lyght & subtyle meates.

The sygnes to knowlege the stomake.

The sygnes of a stomake that is of an yll & weyke dygestyon is whan the body is unlusty, hevy, & slouthfull, the face is swollen, & yaneth often, & hath payne in his eyen, & bolketh often & rudely, & the bolkyng is sowre & unsavery, watry & stynkyng, & therby is bredde wyndes & swellynge of the bely & the appetyte of meate is marde. Therfore swete sone beware of meates and drynkes that may hurte or be contrary to thy helth.

An epystle of grete value.

Moost dere sone Alexander sythe it is so that the body of man is corruptyble by dyversite of complexyon, & of contrary humours that ben in it, wherby often there cometh corrupcyon to it, I thought to delyver the some thyng that shall be necessary & prouffytable to the. In the whiche I wyll treate of the secretes of physyke whiche shall please the. For certayne dyseases come to a kynge whiche be not honest to shewe to physycyens. And yf thou wylt observe this lesson, thou shalt have no nede of physycyens, except in causes that may come in batayle, the whiche may be exchewed. Alexander fayre sone, whan thou rysest frome thy slepe, walke and stretche thy membres egally and combe thy heed, for stretchyng of the lymmes gyveth force, and combynge reyseth the vapoures that ben come in slepynge and putteth them frome the stomake. In somer wasshe thy heed in colde water, whiche shall yelde the naturall heate, and shall be cause of appetyte to meate. Than clothe the with goodly and ryche apparell. For the hert of man delyteth in the beholdyng of precyous meates & clothyng. Than rubbe thy tethe with some cours lynnyn, or other thynge that is hote and drye of compleccyon, and swete of smell for it is holsom for the tethe, and kepeth them clene, clenseth the stenche of the mouth, and clereth the voyce, and gyveth appetyte to eate. And rubbe thy heed often in the same wyse for it openeth the claustres of the brayne, and thycketh the necke and other membres, and clenseth the face and the syght, and prolongeth stowpynge of aege, and amendeth the blode. Also anoynt the somtyme with swete smellynge oyntementes, as the tyme reqyreth, for in suche swetenesse thy hert taketh grete pleasure, & is nourysshed therby. And the spyryt of lyfe taketh refeccyon in good odoures: and the blode renneth meryly thrugh the vaynes of the body. After that take somtyme an electuary of a wood called Aloes, and of Rubarbe whiche is a precyous thynge, to the pryce of foure pens. Which thou shalt fynde wryten in the boke of physyke, and this shall do the moche good, for it voydeth the heate of the mouth of the stomake, and warmeth the body and wasteth wyndes, and maketh good taste and savoure. After this I councell the that thou be often with thy noble and wyse men of thy realme, & speke to them of thy besynesses that thou hast to do. And governe them sadly accordynge to theyr good customes.

Of the maner to travayle.

Or ever thou eate or thyn appetyte cometh at thyne houre accustomed do som travayle, that is to wyte walke or ryde a lytell, or do some other worke, for it helpeth the body moche, it voydeth all ventosytees, and maketh the body lyghter, stronger and lustyeth the stomake, and wasted evyll humoures of the body and maketh the flewme of the stomake descende.

Of the maner of eatynge.

Fayre sone whan thy meate is set afore the, eate of suche as thou desyrest moost, resonably, with well levayned breed. And eate [fyrst] of such as ought to be fyrst eaten. For there be to maners of dygestyon of meat in a man that is to wyte, softe, & harde. For in the botom is moost heat for to make [dygestion of] meate, bycause it is moost flesshly, and nyghest the heat of the lyver wherwith the meate is soden and dygested.

Of abstynence of meat.

Whan thou eatest, eate by leasure, though thou have grete sppetyte to eate. For yf thou eate gredely noughty humoures do multyply, the stomake is laden, the body is greved, the hert is hurte, and the meate remayneth in the stomakes botome undygested.

How pure water ought not to be drunken.

Also beware dere sone that ye drynke no pure water, specyally whan thou haste eaten meate. But yf thou be wont therto. For as soone as the water is upon the meate, it coleth the stomake, and quencheth the heate of the dygestyon and comforte of the meat. It letteth dygestyon and greveth the body. Yf thou must nede drynke water alone, take it the most temperately, and as lytell as thou mayst.

Of the maner to slepe.

Whan thou hast taken thy refeccyon and hast luste to slepe, lye downe on a softe bedde and slepe temperatly. And fyrst lye downe on the lyfte syde, and slepe theron a reasonable space, for the lyfte syde is colde and hath nede to be warmeth. And yf thou fele ony payn in thy bely or in thy stomake, than lay therto a soverayne medycyne, that is a warme lynnen cloth layde theron. Wyte thou dere sone that travayle is good, and gyveth heate to the stomake. But after dyner it is a noughty thynge, for the meate abydeth undygested in the botome of the stomake, and therof be bredde many dyseases. And slepe before fedynge is not good, for it maketh the body leane and dryeth the humoures. But slepynge after fedynge is good, for it fulfylleth the body & gyveth force, & nourysshyng therto. For whan the body of man resteth, than the natural heat draweth the heat that was spredde in all the membres in to the botom of the stomake, & syveth strength therto upon the refeccyon of the meat. And heat requyreth rest. Therfore some phylosophres have sayd that it is better & holsomer to eat at nyght than in the mornyng, for the eatyng in the mornynge bycause of the heat of the day greveth the stomake, & the body is more travayled therwith. And moreover the person shauffeth in travaylyng doynge his besynesse, in goyng & spekyng, & many other thynges that belongeth to the body of man, by the which heat that is outwarde towarde none, the naturall heat that is inwarde is weyked & appeyred, & the meate is harde to dygest. But at nyght it is more easy & lesse greved with the heat of traveyle. And the hert & membres of man ben more in quyet by the coldnesse of the nyght, that gyveth naturall heat to the stomake.

The kepyng of custome or wont.

Thou shalt understande my dere sone that he that is wonte to eate but one meale often is dyseased, for the stomake is without dygestyon & the body hath smal nourysshyng. And he that is accustomed to eate at one time ones another tyme twyse he shal lyghtly preveve that it doth hym harme, for custome chargeth nature.

How one ought to chaunge custome.

And yf nede constreyne the to chaunge thy custome, do it wysely, that is to wyte by lytel and lytell. And so by the grace of god thy chaungynge shall be good. But above al thynges beware that thou eate not tyle thou fele thy stomake empty and that it hath made good dygestyon of the fyrst meale. And this thou mayst knowe by the desyre that thou shalt have to thy meate: and by thy spatle that tornyth subtylly in thy mouthe. And yf thou eate without nede or appetyte the heate of thy stomake shall be made colde as yse. And yf necessyte be that thou must eate, & have an appetyte therto, the kynde heate of thy stomake wyll be as hote as fyre, & of good dygestyon. And beware that whan thy appetyte cometh that thou eate not forth with, for it wyll gadre yll humours of thy body in to thy stomake, whiche wyll hurte thy brayne. And yf thou tary over longe or thou eate, it wyl feble thy stomake, & the meate wyll do thy body no good. And yf so be that thou mayst not eate as soone as thy appetyte requyreth, and that thy stomake be ful of yll humours, do so that thou mayst vomyte or thou eate, & after the vomyte take an electuary, & eate surely.

Of the foure seasons of the yere.

Our intencyon is to treate in this boke of the foure seasons of the yeare, with the qualyte, propryete, contraryte, and dyfference of eche of them. And they ben certayne seasons of the yere devyded as foloweth. That is to wyte [fyrst] prym tyme or vere. [Prymtyme or vere begynneth whan the sonne entreth in the sygne of Aries, and lasteth foure score & xiij. dayes, and .xiij. houres, & the fourthe parte of an houre. That is to wyte from the .x. daye in the ende of Marche, to the foure and twenty day of June.] And in this season the dayes & nyghtes ben egall of length. The wether is fayre. The warme wether cometh. The snowes melte, ryvers renne swyft and clere & waxe warme, the moystenesse of the erthe ryseth to the heyght of trees, and causeth them to smel swete. Medowes and graynes sprowte and corne groweth, & all floures take coloure, byrdes ben clothed with newe robes, and enforce them to synge. Trees ben decked with leves and floures, and the landes with sedes. Beestes engendre and all people take strength & lust. The erthe is arayed goodly, & is a fayre bryde clothed with Jewelles of dyvers coloures bycause she shoulde seme the fayrer at her weddynge.

Of prymtyme, and what it is.

The prymtyme is hote & moyst temperatly as the ayre. This season the blode moeveth and spredeth to all the membres of the body, and the body is parfayte in temperate complexyon. In this season chekyns, kyddes, and poched egges ought to be eaten, with letuses & gotes mylke in these thre monethes. Prymetyme begynneth whan the sonne entreth the syne of Aryes and lasteth .xcii. dayes, an houre and a halfe fro the .x. day of Marche to the .x. day of June. In this season is the best letyng of blode of ony tyme. And than is good to travayle and to be laxatyfe. And to be bathed. And to eate suche thynges as wyll purge the bely. For all dyseases that cometh, eyther by purgyng or bledynge, retorneth anone in this prymetyme.

Of somer, and what it is.

Somer begynneth whan the sonne entreth the fyrst poynt of the crevyce, & lasteth .xcii. days, & an houre & a half. That is to wyte fro the .x. day of June to the .x. day of september. In this season the days be longe, & the nyghtes short. And in al regyons encreaseth & abateth theyr heate & the see is calme, & the ayre meke & fayre. The flours wyther & serpentes encrease & shed theyr venym, & sprede theyr strengyh. The myghtes of mannes body be fortyfyed. And al the world is ful of welth, as the fayre bryde that is goodly stature & in perfyte aege. The season of some hote & drye, & than coler is moeved. And in this season is good to beware of all thynges that be hote & drye of complexyon. And take hede of to moche eatyng or drynkynge for therby is the kyndly heate quenched. In this season eate meates of colde & moyst complexyon, as veale, mylke with vyneygre, & potages made with barly meale. Eate fruyt of eygre savour, as pommegarnets, & drynke small wynes, & use not the company of women. In this season lete the not blode, but yf grete nede compell the. Use lytell travayle, & seldome bathynge.

Of Autompne, or hervest.

Hervest entreth whan the sonneth fometh in to the fyrst degre of the balaunce & lasteth .xci. dayes & an houre & a halfe. That is to wyte fro the .x. daye of Septembre to the x. daye of Decembre. In this season the day & nyght be of one length. And than the dayes waxe short & the nyghtes longe. The ayre is derke, & the wyndes entre the northern regyons or septentryon. The wether chaungeth, & the ryvers & sprynges waxe lesse. The orcheyardes & fruytes wydreth. The beaute of erthe fadeth. Byrdes cease theyr syngyng. Serpentes seke theyr holes wher they assembled theyr lyvyng in somer for the tyme of wynter. The erthe is as an olde naked woman that gooth fro youth to aege. This season of hervest is colde & drye, this tyme blacke coler is moeved. In this season is good to eate meates that be hote & moyst as chekyns, lambe, & drynke olde wynes, eate swete reasyns. And kepe the from all thynges that brede blacke coler, as lyenge with women more than in somer, nor bath ye not but yf grete nede requyre it to be done. In this season yf a man have nede of vomytynge, do it at none in the hotest of the day. For at that tyme all the superfluytees of mannes body gadreth togyder. Also it is good to purge the bely with a medycyn ordeyned therfore & other thynges that ben to expulce blacke coler & to refrayne humoures.

Of wynter, and what it is.

Wynter cometh whan the sonne entreth the fyrst degre of the sygne of Caprycorne & lasteth lxx. dayes & an houre & a halfe. And begynneth the .x. day of Decembre, and contynueth to the .x. daye of Marche. In this season the nyghtes be longe & the dayes short; it is veray colde. The wynes be in the presse, & the leves fall, & herbes leeseth all theyr strength, or the moost parte. All bestes hydeth them in caves and pyttes of hylles. The ayre and the wether is darke. And the erthe is lyke as olde decrypyte persone, that by grete aege is naked and nygh to the deth. Wynter is veray colde and moyst, & than behoveth the use hote meates, as chekyns, hennes, motton, and other hote & fatte flesshe, eate fygges, nuttes, and drynke grene wynes. And beware of to moche laxe and bledynge, & eschewe company of women, for it wyll feble thy stomake, and bathes be good. And for the grete colde the natural heate entreth in to the body, and therfore the dygestion is better in wynter than in somer. And in hervest the bely is colde, and than the poores ben open by heate of the season, and reproveth the naturall heate of all the partes of the body. And therfore the stomake hath but lytel heate, wherby the dygestyon is febled, and the humours assemble there.

Of naturall heate.

Sone Alexander I pray the kepe the kyndly heate of thy body, and thou shalt have longe helth. For the body of man dyeth in .ii. maners. One is by grete aege the which overcometh the body and dystroyeth it. The other is accydentally, as by wepen, sykenesse, or other adventure.

Of thynges that fatteth the body.

Ryght dere sone these ben thynges that fatteth the body. That is to wyte ease of the body and fyllynge it with deynty meates and drynkes, & mylke, and than to slepe on a soft bed. All swete smellynge floures in theyr season, and bathynge in fresshe waters. But yf thou bathe the, tary not longe in it, and have swete smellynge thynges in the bath. And never drynke wyne but it be well tempered with water. And specyally in wynter make water of floures called Assynini and put it in to thy wyne, for it is hote of nature. And in somer use vyolettes and floures of malowes & other thynges that be colde, & use to vomyte ones in a moneth specyally. For vomytes wassheth the body and purgeth it of wycked humoures and stynke that is in it. And yf there be but fewe humoures in the stomake, it conforteth the naturall heate. And whan thou hast vomyte wyllyngly, the body wyll fyll it with good humydyte and be of good dysposycyon to dygest. And yf thou governe the thus, thou shalt be mery at thy hert, lusty with reasonable helth and good understandyng, glory & honour, & over all thyn enemyes vyctory. Also I wyll that thou delyte in the beholdyng of goodly persones, or in redynge of delectable bokes, or in weryng of precyous garmentes, and goodly Jewelles, as the tyme requyreth.

Of thynges that leaneth the body.

These ben the thynges that maketh the body to be leane, weyke, and drye: to moche eatyne, to moche travelynge, to moche walkynge in the sone, to moche goyng, to moche slepyng afore noone, melancoly, feare, to bathe in water of the nature of brymstone, eatynge salt meates, to moche drynkynge of olde wyne, to be to laxe, and overmoche letyne of blode. For Ypocras sayth that he that batheth him with a full bely, or lyeth with a woman shal have sykenesse in his entrayles. And also to renne, or to ryde, or to moche travayle after meat bredeth a grete dysease called palsey. And moche eatyng of fysshe, or mylke and wyne togyder Ypocras sayth it wyl make one lazar.

Of the fyrst parte of the body.

Of the .iiij. partes of the body the head is the fyrst. For in the heed gadreth all superfluytees, and evyll humoures, whiche thou shalt fele and knowe by these sygnes folowyng. The eyes ben troubled, the heryng is thycked & the nosestrylles ben stopped. Yf thou fele suche a dysease take an herbe called wormwood, and sethe it in swete wyne tyll the halfe be wasted, than holde it in thy mouth & wasshe it many tymes therwith tyl thou fele that it dooth the good, & eate whyte mustard sede powdred with thy meate. And yf thou do not thus thou mayst happen to have som dysease, & specyally in thyn eyes, in thy brayn, & in other partes of thy body.

Of the seconde parte of the body.

The seconde parte of the body is the bulke. Yf dysease come there thou shalt knowe it by these sygnes folowynge. The tongue is lette, the mouthe is salt, bytter, & unsavery. The mouth of the stomake is sowre with grefe in all thy membres. It behoveth the to eate but lytel & to vomyte, than eate a lytel sugre of roses with aloes & take good comfortyng spyces & eate an electuary named Dionisium. And yf thou do not thus, thou mayst fal in dysease of the syde, of the raynes, & fevers, & specyally of the tongue wherby thou shalt not properly speke, & dyvers other maladyes. Decoccyon of ysope is good.

Of the thyrde parte of the body.

The thyrde parte of the body is the wombe, yf it be combred with evyll humoures thou shalt knowe it by these sygnes. The bely wyll swell with payne & styfnesse in the knees goynge a slowe pace. It behoveth to use some subtyle & lyght meates, as is sayd before with the governynge. And yf thou do not thus there wyl folowe ache in the hyppes, in the mylte, in the back, and other ioyntes, and in the lyver, with yll dygestyon.

Of the fourthe parte of the body.

The fourth parte of the body ben the genytours. Yf superfluyte & noughty humoures gadre in them thou shalt knowe it by these sygnes. The appeytye wyl waxe colde, & reednesse wyll appere upon them & upon the share. Than must thou take a sede called Apij with fenell sede & the rote of mugwort, & of another called Acham, & atracies. And with these herbes put the rotes in good whyte wyne, & drynke a quantyte of it every mornyng with a lytell water & hony & eate not moche after it. And yf thou do not thus thou shalt have payne in the bladder, & lyver, & shalt not pysse, & shalt have grefe in the intrayles and lunges with brekynge of the stone. Swete sone Alexander I have rede also the hystoryes of a myghty kynge, whiche assembled all the best phylosophres that were in Ynde and Grece. And commaunded them to make a medycyne so prouffytable that he sholde nede none other for his helth. The Grekes sayd he that drynketh every morning twyse his mouthfull of warme water shall have a good ende, and shall nede none other medycyne. The physycyens of Ynde sayd that it is good to eate every day fastyng a quantyte of greynes of whyte hony. And me semeth that who so taketh one of these sayd medycynes by reason shall not have payne in his wombe, nor ought not to feare palsey, nor gowte, nor ache in his Joyntes. And who so eateth every mornyng .vij. dragmas of clustres of swete wyne grapes, shall not feare the dysease of flewme, and it wyll amende his mynde, and claryfy his understandynge, and he nedeth not to doubt fever quartaynes. And who so eateth in the mornynge a fygge with nuttes and a quantyte of leves of rue, that day shall not nede to feare venym.

Of naturall heate.

Moost myghty kynge I requyre the to study the maner to kepe the naturall heate of thy body, with the moysture therof, in the which two thynges lyeth the helthe of thy persone. And knowe thou that the destruccyon of the body cometh in two thynges, one is naturall, and the other agaynst nature. And for the contraryte of the complexyon of man, and whan aege surmounteth the body it behoveth for to dye. Other wyse unnaturally by adventure, as by wepen, or stones, or by sykenesse and lacke of helpe, or by venym, and other chaunces.

Of the qualytees of meates.

Forthermore it is good that thou knowe the nature of meates, for some ben grosse, or cours, & some ben lyght & subtyle. The subtyle bredeth thynne blode, & good, as pure wheate, chekyns, & new layde egges. Grosse meates ben good for suche as ben of hote humoures, labourers, fastyng, and that slepe after meales. Meane meates bredeth no hote nor superfluous humours, as the flesshe of lambes, yonge porke, & other that ben hote and moyste, but suche meates chaunge often in rostynge to hardnesse, to heate, and dryenesse. And they ought to be eaten forthwith after the fostynge, and ben good yf they be so taken with good spyces. Some meates brede melancoly, as befe, cowes flesshe, and all flesshe that is cours and drye. Other that brede and fede in moyst and watry, & shadowy places ben more subtyle, better and holsomest.

Of the nature of fysshe.

Fysshes that ben of small substaunce, & thynne skynnes, easy of eatynge, bredde in rennynge waters nyghe the see ben better & lyghter than they that bredde in the see or fresshe ryvers. But fysshe that bredeth in the see is holsomer than fresshe ryver fysshe. Therfore beware of fysshe of grete substaunce with harde skynnes for suche ben comynly venemous.

Of the nature of waters.

Thou ought to knowe that clere renynge waters that ben nyght to cytees in pure grounde as small brokes be the best and lyghtest. Water that cometh out of stony erthe where as is moche fumosytees is hevy, contagyous, & noysom. Water of puddles or fenne full of frogges, addres, and other venymous wormes be unholsom. The sygnes of good water is to be clere, lyght, & of good colour, that lyghtly dooth sethe and lyghtly coole. In suche waters nature delyteth. Salt water of the see is fumysshe and laxeth the wombe, & water of the see is hote and hevy bycause is moeveth not, & the sonne is dayly over it, and it bredeth coler, and creaseth the mylt and the lunges. The drynkynge of waters with a colde stomake fastynge afore dyner greveth the body, and quencheth the heate of the stomake. But drynkynge of water after dyner warmeth the stomake and bredeth flewme. And moche of it corrupteth the meate in the stomake. Thou oughtest to drynke colde water in somer and warme water in wynter, and not contrary wyse. For warme water in somer mollyfyeth and weyketh the stomake, and wasteth the appetyte. And in wynter colde water quencheth the heate, and destroyeth the instrumentes of the brest, it noyeth the lyghtes and lunges and bredeth many greves.

Of the nature of wyne.

The nature of wyne that groweth on mountaynes nygh to the sonne is dryer than that, that groweth on the playne grounde, in moyst places, & shadowes. Wyne is good for aeged people, and such as by moyst & flewmy. And enoyeth them that be yonge and hote. And wyne warmeth & delyvereth colde and cours superfluytees. The reeder and thycker that wyne is the more it bredeth blode. But yf it be stronge and bytter, than it is called the fyrst blode and the fyrst nourysshyng, and hath the nature of drynke and medycyne. And often dronken it noyeth the body and nouryssheth it not. And whan wyne is naturally swete, it noyeth the stomake with smellynges and wyndes, but such wyne is comynly swete of complexyon, and suche as groweth in large feeldes stretchynge towarde the mountaynes and valees havynge swete clustres, & rype, and be not gathred tyll the myght of the substaunce of the bery is gone with the moystnesse, and that the vyne and the grape be somewhat wydred. And thou shalt knowe that wyne ought to be of an eygre taste sharpe and pleasaunt, and have thycke lyes on the botome of the vessell, and fayre and clere above, & whan thou hast fayre and good wyne drynke temperatly therof to the ease of thy body, as the tyme requyreth. For it strengtheneth the stomake and the heates of the body, and helpeth dygestyon and kepeth frome corrupcyon, and rypeth the meate in the membres, puryfyeng it, & worketh in them tyll it be conjunct in good blode, & nourysshynge, and travayleth and reyseth the heat of the body temperately. And kepeth a man sure of wycked humours, it gladdeth the hert, & maketh fresshe colour in the face. It quyckeneth the mynde & soupleth the tongue, & destroyeth all melancoly, & make a man bolde, & to have good courage & appetyte. And hath many other good propryetees. But yf wyne be outrageously taken many inconvenyences come therby. It troubleth the brayne, the mynde, the wyttes, the understondynge. It maketh the vertue of natural heate wylde, & causeth forgetfulnesse. It combreth the tongue & weyketh all the synewes & lymmes of the body. It maketh the eyes reed & blered.

It chaungeth the colour, & destroyeth the body, & maketh cours & noughty blode. It marreth dygestyon. It causeth to many wordes, & to moche slepe. It maketh the mouth stynkynge. It letteth the goynge, & dystroyeth the sede of man & bredeth lepry, Beware therfore that thou drynke not wyne outrageously, but moeve & chaunge the nature therof with rewbarbe which causeth the lyver to lyve. And wyne with Rubarbe hath many vertues as is founde playnly in bokes of physyke. Howbeit Rubarbe & wyne be bothe deedly venym yf they be outragyously taken. And surely all evyls cometh of wyne unmeasurably dronken.

Of goodnesse & harme that cometh of wyne.

Noble kynge Alexander, forgete not to take tarte syropes in the mornyng fastynge when flewmatyke humours habounde to moch. For it is proufytable & wasteth them moche. Also I mervayle that ony man may dye or be seke that eateth breed of clene and good wheat, holsome & good flesshe, & drynketh good wyne of grapes temperatly. And yf he kepe hym fro to moche drynkyng, eatyng, & travayle. Yf sykenesse overcome such a man he must be healed as a dronken man. That is to wyte he must be wasshed with warme water, and than set over a rennyng water betwene .ii. grene wylowes, & his stomake anoynted with an oyntement of sandres, or sandalles, & have a fumygacyon of frankensence: & other swete spyces, & it wyl do him hoch good. And yf ony man wyll forsake holly the drynkyng of wyne he ought not to leave it sodeynly at ones but lytel & lytell, & to mengle it every day with water more & more, tyll at the last there be nothynge but clere water. And so he may kepe his helth & good complexyon. Thus governe thy body yf thou wyll lyve longe. And kepe my doctrynes, & consydre these thynges folowynge wherein nature conforteth gretely. That is to wyte: Goodly pastymes, syght of grete rychesses, grete reverence, vyctory over enemyes, fedyng on good meates, noyse of mynstralsy, syght of precyous garmentes, often herynge of good tydynges, speche of wyse men, to enquere of thynges past and to come, and communycacyon with fayre gentylwomen.

Of the fourme of Justyce.

O moost dyscrete kynge Justyce can not be praysed to moche, for it is of mervaylous sharpe nature, lyke to the moost gloryous god. And he ordeyned it over his aungels, over his werkes, & over al realmes. And thou ought to kepe Justyve, and defende the wyttes, the rychesses, & possessyons of thy subgectes and all theyr werkes, for so dooth almyghty god. And ony lorde aoyng in lyke case is lyke to god. For by maynteyning of Justyce he foloweth god, and thou ought to folow hym in all nedefull werkes. And this is the fourme of understandynge the whiche god created, and graunted to his creatures. By Justyce the erthe was made, and kynges ordeyned to kepe and maynteyne Justyce, for it maketh subgectes meke and obedyent, prowde men lowly, and kepeth all persons in saufe fro wronges and domages. And therfore they of Ynde saye that the Justyce of a good lorde is better than the rayne that falleth in the evenyng. And there was once founde wryten in a stone in the speche of Caldee that wyse kynges ben bretheren havyng nede eche of other, and one maye not be without the other. For all the kynges of the worlde be to rule, and maynteyne Justyce, whiche is the helthe of Justyce. Therfore yf thou hast ony thyng for to do aske councell, for thou arte but one man. And shewe not all thy courage to thy councelers nor lete them not knowe what is in thy wyll to do. For yf thou shew thy mynde at the begynnynge thou shalt be dyspraysed. Than attempre thyn herte, and thy wyll, but here councel fyrst. And manyfeste not that, that lyeth at thy herte tyll thou come to put it in effecte. Consydre well the councell of every man, and whiche of them hath Juged thy mater and counceled the best for the, and with the best love that he hath towards that. And whan thou hast thus recorded thy councell, put thy mynde in effecte without delay. For the gretest destruccyon that may come to a kynge is to be slowe in his werkes and to lese tyme. And yf so be that a yonge man of small estate gyve the good councell, dyspyse it not, for it is possyble that a man may be borne in suche constellacyon that naturally he shall have wysdome.

Example.

There was upon a tyme a chylde borne in the partyes of Ynde. In the hous where this chylde was borne were certayne wyse men lodged, whiche founde that the sayd childe was borne under such a constellacyon, planet, and sygne that he sholde be wyse, meke, courteys, amyable, fresshe of wytte, and sholde be loved of kynges & grete lordes. Whiche thynge they wolde not shew to the fader which was a wever. When the chyld came to aege the fader & moder set hym to theyr occupacion, but he coude never lerne for ony beatyng nor chastysement. At the last they lete him do as he lyst, & he set his mynde to lerne scyences, & the moevynges of the skyes, & of all thynges above nature. Also he lerned good condycyons & maners to the governaunce of prynces & kynges. And fynally by his wytte & wysdome he was ruler of all the countre.

Another example.

In the realme of Ynde were .ii. chyldren. Whan one of them came to aege the kyng set hym to scole for to lerne scyence, & all the studyes of Ynde & had the best techers in all the provynces for to teche him in all the spede that coude be possyble as to a kynges sone belonged. But all the dylygences of his fader and other techers avayled nothynge nor coude make hym enclyne neyther by his mayster nor by his nature to lerne ony scyence nor arte but onely forgynge or smythes crafte, wherof the kynge merveyled, and sore troubled sent for all the wysest of his realme, and demaunded of them how it myght be that his sone wolde lerne nothynge but onely smythes craft. And they answered that the kynde of the chylde was of suche complexyon, and that he was inclyned to that arte and to none other.

Therefore dere sone Alexander dyspyse no man of lowe byrthe nor of small stature yf thou se ony scyence or ony wysdome in hym, and that he have also cood condycyons and maners in hym, and dooth exchewe vyces. Suche one so wel manered is worthy to be loved of prynces and kynges. And thou ought for to do nothynge without councell. And I pray the dere sone that thou love hym that loveth trouthe & that counceleth the faythfully & somtyme contrary to thyn opynyon. For suche a man is stedfast of courage, faythfull & Just to the & thy subgectes. And the councel of such a man is good to the governayle of the kynge & of his realme. Forthermore lette not thy besynesses that sholde by fyrst done be the last, &c., But do every thynge by councell & ordre. For councell is the shewer of all thynges to come. It is behoveful therfor that thou do all thy werkes by councell of faythfull & secrete councelers. For thy wysdom by the councell of them shall encrease, as the see encreaseth by the ryvers & floodes that fall in to it. And the better thou mayst wynne by the myght of warryours. It is founde wryten that a grete wyse man of Ynde wrote lettres to his sone in this wyse: `My well beloved sone, it is behovefull that thou beleve councell in all thy besynesses, for thou

arte but one man. Take councel therfore of suche as thou knowest
can gyve the good. And above all thynges spare not thy enmy, but
whan thou mayst shew thy vyctory over hym. And ever be ware of
the power of thy enmy. Trust not in thy owne wytte nor in the
grete heyght of thyn estate, but ever take councel of other, which
yf thou seme good & prouffytable accepte it, & elles not. And also
I admosest the & councell the chefely that thou never make none
of thy offycers thy lyeftenaunt onely, nor gyve hym thy myght, for
his councel may destroy the, thy realme, & thy subgectes. And
seke alway to his own prouffyt & thy undoyng. But thou ought to
have dyvers offycers, & yf thou wyll assay and prove ony of them
thou must fayne that thou hast grete nede of money. And yf he
councel the to take of thy treasure & Jewelles for to spende he
loveth the and is faythful to the. And yf he councell the to take
the money of thy subgectes to make them poore he is corrupte &
hateth the moche. But yf he be such one that wyl offre the his
own goodes and say, ``Syr by the gyfte and grace of god I have
goten some goodes I gyve them to the," suche ought to be praysed
and loved best, as he which had lever to gyve his goodes awaye
than the poore subgectes sholde be taxed and destroyed. Prove
also thy offycers and yf thou se that ony of them dooth his offyce
dylygently, and more for thyn honoure than he is commytted,
thou ought gretly to trust in hym. And yf there be ony that
delyteth in takyng of gyftes and gapeth for promocyon, & to
gadre treasure, put not thy trust in hym. For suche a man is lyke a
hurle pytte without botome, for the more that he hath the more
he coveyteth to have. And suche one is the destruccyon of a
realme many wayes. For peradventure the brennynge desyre that
he hath to gete rychesses maye moeve hym to many evylles, and
maye chaunce the procuracyon of thy deth. Yf thou perceyve
suche an offycer, lete hym not be ferre frome thy presence. And
suffre hym not to make treaty with straunge lordes nor prynces,
nor wryte no newes to them. And yf thou doubt that he dooth
the contrary, chaunge him without ony delay. For the courage of
many men be soone chaunged, and lyghtly inclyned to do
contrary thynges.' Also dere sone thou ought to cherysshe the

offycer that loveth and moeveth thy subgectes to love the. And that putteth his persone and goodes to thyn honoure, and that hath these propryetees folowynge. that is to wyte that he be parfyt in his lymmes for to travayle in his offyce that he is chosen to. That he be courteys, lowly, and eloquent, and that his worde accorde with his hert. That he be a clerke wyse & well condycyoned, laborous & sober of mouthe in eatynge and drynkynge, not lecherous, nor player at dyce and other dysordynate games. That he be hardy, and set not his mynde on golde nor sylver, nor other thynge of the worlde, but that, that belongeth to the governaunce of the, and the realme. That he love the welth of his neyghbours as of them that be ferre. And that he hate all wronges, and by Justyce yelde every man his owne. That he be angry with them that do injuryes & extorcyons, & that he greve no man wrongfully. And that he be perseveraunt & stedfast in his purpose which is behovefull. That he be without feare and in good wyll. That he knowe the stynte of his expences. And that he prolonge nothynge that may be prouffytable to the realme. And that gyveth not thy subgectes cause to complayne of hym in doynge agaynst the comyn wele. That he be not ful of wordes, nor a grete laugher. That none be refused comyng to his hous. And that he be dylygent to here & enquese of newes and tydynges. That he comfort the subgectes and correct theyr werkes, & help them in theyr adversytees.

Of kynges secretaryes.

Dere sone it behoveth to chuse the a secretary for to wryte & knowe thy secretes; he must be a man of grete wysdome and well lerned, for to understande thy mynde. He ought to be trusty and eloquent and that can speke dyvers languages for to put thy besynesses in goodly ordnaunce and semely speche. For as a fayre garment honoureth the body of a kynge, so goodly speche arayeth and indeweth a lettre. And also he must be trusty to hyde & kepe close thy doynges. And that he suffre none to come to the place where thy wrytynges be & that none se them. Swete sone such persones ought to be cherysshed & well rewarded for theyr servyces. And exalte them in suche wyse that they be always dylygent in thy necessytes & nedes. For in them is conteyned thy glory and honour, or thy lyfe & destruccyon.

Of a kynges messagers.

Myghty emperour the messagers alway sheweth the wysdome of hym that sendeth them. They ben the eyes, the eeres, & the mouthe of theyr lord. It behoveth for thy messagers or ambassadours to chuse suche as ben moost suffycyent, of clere understanding, wyse, honourable, & trusty, which loveth thy honour, & hateth thy dyshonour. (For in thy court thou mayst finde them bothe.) And yf thou fynde suche discover & shewe thy courage to them. And if thou fynde none suche or better, fynde one that wyll trustely bere thy lettres, & brynge the an answere of them. And yf thou fynde that messager be covetous to do his owne prouffyte & to gete gyftes, truste not in hym, but entyerly forsake hym. And also make no man thy messager that wyll be dronke, for by suche one it shall be sayd & knowen that the lorde is not wyse. And ferthermore make not thy messager of thy gretest offycer, & lete hym not be ferre from the, for it may well be the undoyng of the & the realme. And yf thou sende messagers by whome ony treason come to the, I tel the not the measure of payne tat they ought to suffre, but do therin as thou semest best.

Of the governaunce of the people.

Fayre sone thou knowest that thy people & subgectes ben the hous of thy mynde, & the treasure wherby thy realme is conforted. For thy realme & subgectes ben as an orchyarde wherin ben dyvers trees berynge fruyte, the which trees have dyvers rotes & sedes for to bere, growe, & multyply the fruyte, & be the defence & durable treasure to thy realme, & of thy myght. It behoveth than that thy subgectes be well governed, & that thou take thought and care to that, that is nedefull for them, and to beware that no vyolence nor wronges be done to them, and after theyr condycyons and wontes to ordre them. Than gyve to them a good offycer that intendeth not to theyr undoynge, but that intendeth to rule them well, Justly and in quyete. And se that suche a good offycer be wyse, full of good maners, well condycyoned, and pacyent. For yf he be not suche one, wyte thou that the wyse men that were good before, wyll become evyll and rebell agaynst the. Also se that thou have good and dyscrete Juges, and that shall be worshyp to the, and encrease of thy court, and of thy realme. And that the sayde Juges be not corrupte with gyftes and mede, and that they have good notaryous scrybes, and egall sollycitours & advocates that wyll not take brybes as it happeneth seldom. Dere sone I pray the and admonest the that thou put thy selfe often in batayle, and take oftentymes the councell of them of thy court. But put the not with them that onely by enve and covetyse entreth presumptuously in batayle. And blame not nor dyspyse thy men of warre, but use fayre wordes amonge them, and often promyse them gyftes and honours. And in no wyse put thy selfe in batayle tyll thou be pourveyed of al necessary armes and other thynges therto belongynge. And whan thou seest thyn enmy renne sodaynly upon hym, and not slowly, and ever have good outryders and watches about thyn hoost. And lodge the alwayes as nyghe as thou mayst to hylles, woodes and waters. And have alway more haboundaunce of vytayle than nedeth. And above al thynges grete quantyte of trompettes, tabours and other mynstrelles. For they gyve force, myght, and rejoyce them that be with the, and make dyvysyon & feare to thyn enemyes. And be not alway armed in one harneys, but with dyvers. And be well stored with archers & handgonnes. And ordeyne some of thy men to renne, and other to stande stedfastly in thy batayles. Conforte thy men with fayre wordes and gyve them courage, & herty them to fyght. And above all thynges dere sone beware of treason with all thy power, and have ever good knyghtes about the well & swyftely horsed that yf chaunce happen that thou must nedes flee, that by them thou mayst save thy persone. But yf thou see ony of thyn enemyes fle haste the not to chase them but kepe thy folke alway togyder the moost that thou mayst. And yf thou wylt assawte castelles or townes have grete quantyte of gynnes, and artyllery for to breke the walles. And pourvey the of connynge myners, and grete nombre of archers and crosbowes. And do soo that thou mayst take away the water from them of the fortresse. And ever kepe some of thy enmyes for to knowe theyr doynges within. And yf thou can not have it but by batayle doo it. For alway the last ende of thy werkes ought to be batayle. And this ought to be done whan thou can not have them otherwyse. And doo all thy werkes by councell and not hastely.

Of the physonomy of people.

Among all other thynges of this worlde I wyll that thou knowe a
noble and mervaylous scyence that is called physonomy by the
which thou shalt knowe the nature and condycyon of people. And
it was founde by a phylosophre named Physonomyas, the whiche
sought the qualytees of the nature of creatures. In the tyme of the
sayde Physonomyas reygned the moost wyse physycyen Ypocras.
And bycause the fame of Physonomyas and his wysdome was so
gretely spredde, the dyscyples and servauntes of Ypocras toke his
fygure secretly, and bare it to Physonomyas to here how he wolde
Juge and say by the sayd fygure of Ypocras. And bade hym say
and tell the qualyte therof. Whan Physonomyas had well
beholden it, he sayd: `This man is a wrangeler lecherous and
rude.' This herynge the dyscyples of Ypocras they wolde have
slayne Physonomyas, and sayd to hym: `Aa fole this is the fygure
of the best man of the worlde.' Whan Physonomyas saw them
thus moeved, he appeased them the best waye that he coude with
fayre wordes saynge. I knowe well that this is the fygure of the
wyse man Ypocras. And I have shewed you by scyence as I knowe.
Whan the dyscyples were come to Ypocras they tolde hym what
Physonomyas had sayd. And Ypocras sayd, `Truely Physonomyas
hath tolde you the trouthe, and hath left nothyng of my
complexyon in the whiche ben all my vyces. But reason in me
overcometh and ruleth the vyces of my complexyon.'

Dere sone I have shortely abreged to the, the rules of this scyence
of Physonomy, the whiche shall infourme the gretely. Yf thou se a
man with salowe coloure, flee his company, for he is inclyned to
the synne of lechery, and to many evylles. Yf thou seest a man
that smyleth lyghtly, and whan thou beholdest hym he wyll loke
shamfastly and wyl blusshe in his face and sygh, with teeres in his
eyes yf thou blame hym for ony thynge, surely he feareth the and
loveth thy persone. Beware of hym as thy enmy that is tokened in
his face, and of hym also that is mysshapen. The best complexyon
that is, is he that is of meane coloure with browne eyes and heere,

and his bysage between whyte and reed, with an upryght body, with a heed of metely bygnesse, and that speketh not but of nede be, with a softe voyce, suche a complexyon is good, and suche men have about the. If the heeres be playne and smothe the man is curteys and meke, and his brayne is colde. Harde heere and curled is a token of foly, & lewdnesse. Moche heere on the brest and on the bely betokeneth very yll or very good complexyon naturally and is very amerous, and kepeth in his herte the injuryes that hath ben done to hym. Blacke heere betokeneth to love reason & Justyce.

Duskysshe eyes betokeneth fooly, & lyghtly to be angry. Gray eyes betokeneth honeste, & lovynge peas. Bygge eyes betokeneth to be envyous, unshamefast, slowe & unobedyent. Eyes meane between blacke and yelowe is of good understanding, curteys, and trusty. Wyde retchynge eyes and a longe face betokeneth a man malycyous and yll. Eyes lyke an asse alway lokyng downe is of harde nature and nought. Waveryng eyes with a long face betokeneth gyle, rennynge mynde and untrusty. Reed eyes betokeneth to be stronge and of a grete courage. He that hath spekles about his eyes, whyte, blacke, or reed, is the worst of all other men. Thycke heered eye lyddes is an yll speker, he that hath them hangynge longe to his eyes, is neyther true nor clene. He that hath heere ynough betwene his two browes and be thynne and not to longe, is of a good and grete understandyng.

A sklendre nosed man is soone angry. A longe nose hawked to the mouthe, is a token of honeste and hardynesse. A snytted nose is a token of a token to be soone vexed. Wyde nosethrylles in a man is slouth and boystousnesse and soone angered. A brode nose in the myddes is a grete speker, and a lyer. But the best is he that is meane neyther to wyde nor to close. The vysage that is ful & flat, and that is not swollen nor to bygge is a token of an yll persone, envyous, injuryous, and a wrangeler. But he that hath a meane vysage of fourme of chekes and eyes, neyther to fat nor to leane, he is trusty, lovynge, and of grete understandynge, wyse and full of servyce and wytte.

He that hath a wyde mouthe loveth batayle and is hardy. He that hath thycke lyppes is folysshe. And he that hath a wrynkled face is a lyer, and careth not of many debates. He that hath a sklender face is of grete reason. He that hath a lytell vysage and yelowe of colour is a deceyver, dronken, and evyll. Full eyes & smothe chekes is soon angry.

Small eeres betokeneth foly, and lechery.

He that hath a small voyce & speketh thycke loveth feyghtynge. He that hath a meane voyce, neyther to bygge, nor to lytell, is folysshe and unreasonable. And he that speketh to moche with a sklender voyce, is not over honest, and of smal care. He that hath a femynyne voyce is soone angry, and of yl nature. A softe voyced man is often angry and envyous. He that hath a fayre voyce, is folysshe, and of hyghe courage. He that speketh lyghtly, lyeth often, and is a deceyver. And he that speketh without moevynge his handes, is of grete wysdome and honeste.

He that hath a sklender necke, is hote, deceytfull, and folysshe. He that hath a grete bely is proude, lecherous, and unwyse.

He that hath a large brest, thycke sholdres, and bygge fyngers, is hardy, wyse, gentyll, and of good wytte. He with a sklender backe agreeth never with ony other. He that hath his brest and backe egall, is a token of honeste. Hye reysed sholdres, is a token of lytell tydelyte, nought, and sharpe. He that hath longe armes rechynge to the knee, is of grete boldenesse, sadnesse, & lyberalyte. Shorte armes betoken that he loveth socour, and is folysshe.

Longe palmed handes with longe fyngers, is ordeyned to lerne many scyences, and artes, and specyal handy craftes, and to be of good governaunce. Fyngers short and thycke, betoken foly.

Shorte thycke fete and flesshy, betokeneth to be folysshe, and full of injury. A lytell lyght fote, is a man of smal understandynge. A sklender fote sheweth a man to be symple, and of small knowlege. He that hath a thycke fote is hardy and folysshe.

The length of the legges, & the heles, betoken strength of the body. A thycke flesshy kne, is soft and weyke.

A man that gooth a grete pace, is wyllynge in all thynges, and to hasty.

He is of a good nature and complexyon, that hath softe flesshe and moyst, meanely smothe and rough, and that is kyndly between reed and whyte.

He that hath a smoothe contenaunce, soft here & playne, with meane eyes of bygnesse, with a well proporcyoned heed, a good necke and suffycyent in length, with sholders somdele lowe, and his legges and knees metely flesshed, his voyce competent clere, the palmes of his handes and fyngers longe, and not thycke, and that he laughe but lytell, and that is no mocker, with a smylyng chere and mery, is of good complexyon. Howbeit dere sone I commaunde the not to Juge all upon one sygne, but consydre all the tokens of a man whiche moost habounde and sheweth the foly in hym, and holde the to the best and moost prouffytable party.

Deo gratias.

Thus endeth the abstract of the secrete of secretes of Arystotle prynce of Phylosophres. Here folowe certayne reasons of the grete phylosophre Sydrac to the kynge Boctus, whiche I have translated out of the Pycardes speche, thynkynge it necessary in this sayd treatyse.

Reasons of the grete phylosophre Sydrac

How one ought to uttre his speche.

Yf thou hast ony mater of gravyte or sadnesse of reason, to shewe and declare before noble and wyse audyence, tell it brevely and wysely, with a good bolde courage and wyll, and than they wyll take it hertely, and wyll gyve credence to thy wordes and alowe thy saynge. For wyse men wyll gladly gyve eeres to wyse and short informacyon. And therfore be nor shamefast nor aferde to tell the trouth. For many one have loste theyr ryght by shamefastnesse and feare of theyr utteraunce of wordes, though theyr causes were good.

The maner of angre.

Thou oughtest not to be angry through thy brother or frende as shew the hevy chere somtyme, for peradventure he hath some cause wherfore he can shew the, nor none other good chere or countenaunce, and so it is with hym. And yf thou hast had ony wordes with ony man, and he shewe the yll countenaunce, therfor yet thou ought not to be angry with hym. For perchaunce he is too lewde or unwytty of hymselfe that he can do no better, and yet he weneth that he doth wel, for ever the lewdest sheweth moost anger. For whan a wyse man is angry, he sheweth it not outwarde by his reason. A man ought more to feare the anger of a wyse man than of a foole, for the wyse man can better revenge his angre than a foole, howbeit that a foles angre is often comberous.

To uttre secretes.

In one maner only thou ought to shew thy secretes, that is to wyte to almyghty god that knoweth al thyng, that is to be understande, to his lyftenaunt in erth, and other wyse not. For yf thou dyscover it to thy frende, and yf thy frende be but lewde, & hath another frende that he loveth, to whome he telleth hym the same, and so frome one to another tyll a grete meyny do knowe it, & so thy secrete may come out to thy grete shame and rebuke. For whyles thou kepest thy secret within the, it is sure. For thou mayst shew thy secrete to suche one that whan he knoweth it wyl do the some wronge, and for feare that thou hast of hym thou dare not gaynsay hym leest he bewrey the. And yf thou can none otherwyse but that thou must uttre it by thy foly, and that thy stomake wyl swell for to tel it, go out of company and tell it to thy selfe as yf thou wolde tell it to another man, and thy hert will coole and thy stomake swage. And for ony nede that thou hast to dyscover it, take hede to whom, but yf it be to suche one that for ony anger that thou doost to hym wyl not rebuke the with it. And hever lete thy neyghboure knowe thy nede, for therby thou mayest be the lesse set by in places where thou dwellest.

How thou oughtest to sporte with thy frende.

Loke wysely how thou playest or bourdest with thy frende (or other) with thy handes or with thy mouth, for yf thou do hym harme, harme may come to the. With sportyng with handes cometh angre and murdre, whyther it be thy brother or frende. For yf thou hurt hym or wryng his hande, or cast hym downe, or smyte hym otherwyse, it shall greve hym, & shame hym in his mynde, albeit that he be lytell and weyke, for eche in hym selfe counteth hym stronge, bolde and fyers, and yet he wyll prayse hym selfe thoughe he be a cowarde and nought. And yf thou mocke hym, thou shalt spyte hym to the hert, for he wyll thynke that thou dyspysest hym, & that thou reputeth hym at nought. And yf thou mocke hym before people, thou doost hym yet more spyte, & he cometh angre and grete hate, though it be thy brother or other frende. But thou ought to pastyme with fayre wordes, and to shewe goodly auctorytees and reasons to drawe theyr love to the, for by that pastaunce thou mayst come to the goodnesse, love and curteysy of people.

The maner to doubt and trust thyn enemy.

Whyther thyn enemy be stronge or weyke, thou ought not to doubt hym to moche, nor trust to moche to hym, for he that is overcome today, may be vyctour tomorow. And he that is vyctour today may be overthrowen to morow. And he that doubteth none, none will have doubt of hym. To moch doubt maketh to moch trust, and to moch trust maketh to moche domage. For he that bereth doubt alwaye with hym, hath a grete burden & payne. And he that trust in hym selfe, bereth his owne domage, and his dethe. For thou ought to doubt whan tyme is to doube, and to trust whan tyme is to trust.

Finis.

Lenvoy and excuse of Robert Coplande the translatour of this boke

In humble maner, and moost due reverence
Tremblynge for drede afore thy soverayne
Yf thy chaunce be to come in presence
Where ony person shall the there retayne
Submytte thy selfe as one that wolde be fayne
His grace to please in al maner degre
And of thy rudenesse for to pardon the.

And where as thou art but as an abstract
As touchynge the auctours compylacyon
Yf I therfore be ony wyse detract
In defaut of thy abrevyacyon
Lay thou the blame in the frensshe translacyon
Whiche I have folowed as nygh as I can
Under correcyon of every wyse man.

Yf ony may dyspyse the language rude
Whiche barayne is, of puryd eloquence
Desyre them that they do not delude
Thy fronsayte mater full of sentence
But in theyr hertes, enprynt thy morall sence,
Which compyled is, by wysdome naturall
Of prudent men, the veray governall.

Where many wedes be in a felde of corne
All though the weders thynk to wede it clene
Some shall remayne, whan the fylde is shorne.
Drawke or cokle, yet there wyll be seen
The fawtes therof, is in the handes and eyen
Lykewyse where many wordes and lettres be

No mervayle is, though I some overse.

Yf by impressyon, ony thynge be amys
In worde, in sence, or in ortography
I you requyre, to mende where the faute is
In the best wyse, it for to Justyfy
For though all be not to your fantasy
In formall maner, do ye it dyscus
Save onely god, nemo est perfectus.

Deo gratias.

Dytee du translateur

Tost ou tard, pres ou loing
A le fort du foible besoing.

Thus undeth the secrete of secretes of Arystotle with the governayle of prynces and every maner of estate with rules of helthe for body and soule very prouffytable for every man, and also veray good to teche chyldren to lerne to rede Englysshe.

[Newly translated & emprynted by Robert Copland at London in the Flete-strete at the sygne of the Rose garlande the yere of our lorde .M.CCCCC.xxviij. the .vij. day of August the .xx. yere of the reygne of our moost dradde soverayne and naturall kynge Henry the .viij. defender of the fayth.]

96